Tasty Treats

Hamburgers
Bad News for Cows

Elaine Landau

THE ROURKE PRESS, INC.

VERO BEACH, FLORIDA 32964

PHOTO CREDITS
Ben Klaffke

EDITORIAL SERVICES
Editorial Directions Inc.

Library of Congress Cataloging-in-Publication Data

Landau, Elaine.
   Hamburgers : bad news for cows / Elaine Landau.
      p. cm. — (Tasty treats)
   Includes bibliographical references.
   Summary: Briefly describes the history of hamburgers, different ways they are enjoyed, and present-day variations.
   ISBN 1-57103-337-8
   1. Hamburgers—Juvenile literature. [1. Hamburgers.] I. Title.

TX749.5.B43 L36 2000
641.3'62—dc21

                                                    00–022394

Printed in the USA

Contents

Hamburgers – an all American favorite.

Hamburgers

Americans love hamburgers. They like them more than hot dogs. Studies prove this. Hamburgers are an all-American food. Presidents and movie stars eat them. So do Little Leaguers. This is a book about hamburgers. That wonderful beef in a bun!

Loved by Little Leaguers as an after game treat.

Hamburger History

Hamburgers actually got their start in Europe. During the thirteenth century, fierce bands of horsemen swept through the **region**. They were the Tartar tribes. These men were ruthless fighters. They were also hearty meat eaters.

This lucky cow was not alive when the Tartar tribes raided villages. Of course people still love hamburgers…

A close-up view of ground beef – the stuff of Steak Tartar.

The men raided villages. They took whatever they wanted. This included any unlucky cow they found. The animal was killed for its meat. They chopped the meat into very small pieces. Then they ate it raw.

As time passed others also ate this dish. They added egg yolk, onions, and garlic to the meat. It was called **steak tartar**. Steak tartar was the grandaddy of the hamburger.

By the eighteenth century, steak tartar was a favorite in both Russia and Germany. It was especially popular in the German town of Hamburg. The Germans later brought the recipe to America. They called it "Hamburg-style steak."

The meat was not served raw anymore. It was made into a **patty** and **broiled**. It looked like a hamburger… but the bun was missing.

Hamburg-style steak was made into patties like these and cooked.

The Great Hamburger Mystery

Who put the burger in the bun? We cannot be sure. Some say it was "Hamburger Charlie." Charlie Nagreen sold food at Wisconsin county fairs. He gave people a way to eat while strolling the fairgrounds. Nagreen put a beef patty between two pieces of bread.

Hamburgers were first made at food stands like this one at a fair.

People still enjoy burgers at fairs.

We may not know who invented the hamburger, but we know that this tender, juicy burger looks great!

Others say Frank Menches of Ohio invented the hamburger. Menches also sold food at fairs. One day he ran out of sausage. So he put beef patties in his sandwiches. Was that the real birth of the burger?

Many other people also said they invented it. But no one knows which story is true. The mystery continues.

Burgers barbecued outdoors taste great.

Hamburgers Today

Today hamburgers are better than ever. There are many ways to make them. Tropical burgers offer a taste of the tropics. Pineapple juice is added to the beef. So are coconut flakes. Some people put chopped salted peanuts in their burger patties. They like the flavor. They also enjoy how these crunchy burgers feel when they chew them.

Top your burgers with what you like best.

In Michigan a restaurant serves The Family Burger. This burger weighs over 5 pounds. It feeds between ten and twelve people.

Hamburgers are cooked different ways as well. They may be grilled, broiled, steamed, or fried. People top off their burgers with all kinds of things. Ketchup, cheese, mayonnaise, and pickles are good. Burgers with onions, mushrooms, or **avocados** are tasty, too. Some people even like peanut butter and bananas on their burgers!

Fast-food restaurants sell billions of burgers each year. That is enough to go to the moon and back many times! Many Americans have grown up on hamburgers. Others are still eating and growing.

Fast food restaurants sell many burgers.

But can you talk about hamburgers without mentioning french fries? Some feel that french fries are a hamburger's best friend. Restaurants have paired them through the years. Burgers and fries are served just about everywhere. And french fries are also often a part of packaged hamburger meals for kids. This is especially true at fast food places.

French fries got their start in France. You probably guessed that from their name. Thomas Jefferson tried them when he visited France. He liked them so much that he wanted to enjoy them here. So he brought the recipe back with him. Before long french fries were being served at Monticello. That was Jefferson's home in Virginia. His guests liked them. Soon others began making french fries as well. And in time this French food seemed very American.

Growing up on burgers – part of the fun of being a kid.

Yet today french fries are largely served with hamburgers in restaurants. At home there are usually other choices. Potato salad is often served with hamburgers at barbeques. So is macaroni salad. Baked beans and potato chips are other common hamburger companions. But no matter what they have with it, burger lovers all agree on one thing. Burgers can't be beat!

Burgers can't be beat!

They Taste Good But…

Hamburgers taste good. But are they good for you? Hamburgers contain protein. They also have calcium and iron. Your body needs these things. But hamburgers also have fat. Too much fat is not good for you.

Low fat ground beef.

A veggie burger and fries.

Now you can get healthier burgers. Some hamburgers are made with **lean** beef. This beef has less fat. There are also fish burgers and chicken burgers. A veggie burger is made mostly from vegetables. It looks just like a hamburger. Some taste a lot like one, too.

These kids love hamburgers.

There are all kinds of burgers. But Americans seem to like hamburgers best. This is especially true of young people. We eat 38 billion hamburgers each year. That is good news for kids. Bad news for cows.

Cows don't like hamburgers.

Glossary

avocados (av uh KAH dohz) – green pear-shaped fruit with a buttery flavor

broil (BROY al) – to cook by applying direct heat

lean (leen) – containing little fat

patty (PAT ee) – a round, flat piece of meat

region (REE juhn) – a specific area or place

steak tartar (stayk TAR tur) – raw ground beef prepared with egg yolk and seasonings

For Further Reading

Kalbacken, Joan. *The Food Pyramid*. Danbury, Connecticut: Children's Press, 1998.

Ling, Mary. *Pirate Cookbook*. New York: DK Publishing, 1997.

Patten, Barbara. *Digestion: Food at Work*. Vero Beach, Florida: Rourke, 1996.

Rockwell, Lizzy. *Good Enough to Eat*. New York: HarperCollins, 1999.

Index